Copyright © text and illustrations Century Hutchinson Ltd 1986

All rights reserved

First published in 1986 by Hutchinson Children's Books Ltd
An imprint of Century Hutchinson Ltd
Brookmount House, 62-65 Chandos Place, Covent Garden, London WC2N 4NW

Century Hutchinson Publishing Group (Australia) Pty Ltd
16-22 Church Street, Hawthorn, Melbourne, Victoria 3122

Century Hutchinson Group (NZ) Ltd
32-34 View Road, PO Box 40-086, Glenfield, Auckland 10

Century Hutchinson Group (SA) Pty Ltd
PO Box 337, Bergvlei 2012, South Africa

Designed by Sarah Harwood
Edited by Sarah Ware

Set in Stymie Light, by The Keystroke Mill
Printed and bound in Italy

British Library Cataloguing in Publication Data
Hunt, Roderick, *1939-*
Worm plans a great escape.
I. Title II. Gordon, Mike
823'.914[J] PZ7

ISBN 0 09 167230 9

WORM
plans a great escape

Written by Rod Hunt
Illustrated by Mike Gordon

Hutchinson
London   Melbourne   Auckland   Johannesburg

'It's not fair,' said Worm. 'No-one seems to realise just how useful worms are. We spend our lives digging and churning away under the earth to make it soft and rich, then end up getting picked on or eaten!'

His little body shook with rage. 'Birds, moles, hedgehogs,' he went on. 'We are just breakfast and supper to them, you know.'

'Then don't stand for it,' said Cat. 'I wouldn't. Dogs often chase me, but they soon give up when I stick up for myself.'

'Hmm, I wonder?' muttered Worm.

Worm thought about what Cat had said as he burrowed under the earth the next day.

Suddenly, something hard and sharp closed round his neck and began to pull him out of the ground.

It was the moment he had dreaded.

Worm thought, 'I don't want to end up as a snack in a bird's tummy. Why should I?' So he hung on as Bird pulled and tugged.

Then he shouted, 'Get off!' in such a loud, fierce voice that Bird let go at once and flew away in surprise.

'Well I never!' said Worm, as he returned to his normal length. 'Cat was right.'

Just then, Snail came along. 'Hello,' he said. 'You're looking pleased with yourself.'

'I've good reason to,' said Worm, and he told Snail exactly what had happened.

Spider, overhearing Worm's story, said, 'Do you mean Bird just let you go?'

'Yes,' replied Worm. 'Here I am, alive and wriggling, apart from a little bruising round my neck. Don't you see, if we all stood up for ourselves our lives would be much happier.'

So Worm called a meeting to tell his friends the news.

'Worm Mates, Comrade Snails and Spider Friends,' he declared. 'I am here to tell you all how we can make our lives happier. We must stand up for ourselves.'

'Creatures who think they can just come along and eat us must think again.'

'Try telling that to Mole,' said one of the worms. 'He was snuffling round for a worm supper again last night.'

'All right,' said Worm, 'we *will* tell him.'

That night, when Mole was out hunting, Worm and his friends hid in Mole's tunnel, waiting for him to return.

At last, Mole wheezed and puffed into view. 'Ah, some tasty worms,' he muttered.

'No we're not,' shouted Worm, angrily.

'I beg your pardon,' Mole uttered, astonished.

'We're not tasty,' said Worm, 'and we're not here to be eaten. It must stop!'

'I didn't think you minded being eaten,' said Mole. 'You've not complained before. I'll go. Sorry, I'm sure,' he added.

'It's all very well taking on Mole,' said Snail the next day. 'How about Hedgehog? There's a prickly customer to deal with.'

'I've been thinking about her,' replied Worm, 'and I have an idea. But you will all have to help me.'

Under a bush nearby was an old plastic funnel and a bit of old tube. Worm needed both for his plan. Snail was worried.

'How will you carry them?' he asked.

'Worm power,' said Worm, briskly. 'You snails and spiders can help, too.'

They heaved and grunted and slowly moved the bits from under the bush. Then they practised all the things Worm told them to do.

The next day Spider brought news that Hedgehog was coming. 'Right, team!' Worm called. 'Away we go!'

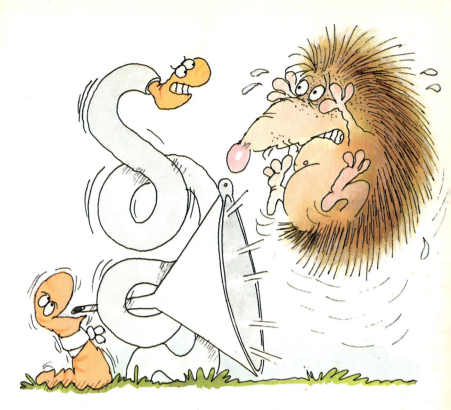

Worm's plan worked perfectly. Hedgehog no sooner began to look for snails and worms than a giant worm appeared in front of her.

'Leave snails and worms and spiders in peace,' boomed a loud voice. 'Or else!'

Hedgehog was so scared, she fled.

A few days later, Worm met Cat and told her how he had stood up to Bird, Mole and Hedgehog. 'Thanks to your good advice we are all alive and well,' he said.

'I'm pleased,' said Cat, 'but I've come to warn you of something far worse.'

'Oh,' said Worm, 'and what's that?'

'A fisherman,' said Cat, urgently. 'I've just seen one digging for worms. You won't be able to stand up to a human, so watch out. Before you know it you'll be dangling on the end of a fishing line.'

Worm thanked Cat and wriggled off rapidly to warn the others.

On the way he passed Snail who said, 'Oh Worm, something really terrible has happened. Look!' He pointed towards a large bucket. 'It's full of worms,' he sobbed. 'They've been dug up.'

'We've got to do something at once!' said Worm. 'Get every snail and spider you can. We've got to set those worms free!'

The spiders and the snails came as quickly as they could. Worm organised them into groups, told them what to do then shouted, 'Right, heave!'

The bucket wobbled, the bucket rocked and then suddenly it tipped over with a crash and the worms spilled out.

'Well done, everyone,' they all cheered.

'We're not out of trouble yet,' said Worm.

'The fisherman may soon be back. Our only hope is to escape. If we all go alone, we won't make it. Together we stand a chance. I have a plan.'

'Tell us, tell us,' cried the worms.

'No time for that. Just do as I say. We must cling together and make a ball.'

It was not easy forming a ball and in the end Worm, who was bigger and stronger than the others, tied himself into a knot and held everyone together from the middle.

'Now push,' called Worm to the snails and spiders. The ball edged forwards.

The worm ball gathered speed. Faster and faster, it rolled down the hill.

'Whee!' shouted the worms. 'This is fun.'

The ball whizzed to the bottom of the hill and broke apart on a bump. The worms all laughed with excitement.

But Worm didn't laugh. He groaned. He was tied in such a tight knot that he couldn't undo himself.

'Help!' he cried in pain. 'Help!'

Then the tiniest worm had a bright idea. 'Why don't we tickle Worm untied?' she suggested.

So they all tickled Worm, who squirmed and wriggled and squiggled and giggled until suddenly his knot flew apart.

'Ooh!' sighed Worm. 'Thank you. It's all very well standing up for yourself but sometimes you do need a little help from your friends.'